INDIAN
ARM

INDIAN
ARM

by Hiro Kanagawa
adapted from Henrik Ibsen's *Little Eyolf*

PLAYWRIGHTS CANADA PRESS
TORONTO

Indian Arm © 2016 by Hiro Kanagawa

For professional or amateur production rights, please contact the
publisher.

LIBRARY AND ARCHIVES CANADA CATALOGUING IN PUBLICATION

Kanagawa, Hiro, author
Indian arm / by Hiro Kanagawa.

"Adapted from Henrik Ibsen's Little Eyolf."
A play.

Issued in print and electronic formats.
ISBN 978-1-77091-572-5 (paperback).--ISBN 978-1-77091-573-2 (pdf).--
ISBN 978-1-77091-575-6 (mobi).--ISBN 978-1-77091-574-9 (epub)

I. Title.

PS8621.A486I53 2016   C812'.6   C2016-906579-0
                                      C2016-906580-4

We acknowledge the financial support of the Canada Council
for the Arts, the Ontario Arts Council (OAC), the Ontario Media
Development Corporation, and the Government of Canada for our
publishing activities.

ACKNOWLEDGEMENTS

Indian Arm was commissioned and developed by Rumble Theatre. Additional development under Arts Club Theatre's 2013 ReACT: New Plays in Progress series. Excerpt from "The Lost Island" from *Legends of Vancouver* (1911) by E. Pauline Johnson. The playwright gratefully acknowledges the help and co-operation of Leonard George, Dennis Thomas, and the Tsleil-Waututh Nation in the creation of this play.

Indian Arm was presented by Rumble Theatre from
April 8–18, 2015, at Studio 16 in Vancouver, BC, with the
following cast and creative team:

CAST

Rita: Jennifer Copping
Borghejm and Old Woman: Gloria May Eshkibok
Alfred: Gerry Mackay
Asta: Caitlin McFarlane
Wolfie: Richard Russ

CREATIVE TEAM

Director: Stephen Drover
Production Designer: Drew Facey
Lighting Designer: Conor Moore
Sound Designer: James Coomber
Associate Director: Corey Payette
Stage Manager: Collette Brown
Assistant Stage Manager: Noelle Sediego
Production Manager: Becky Low
Technical Director: Robin Richardson

CHARACTERS

Rita   midforties, a once-promising combination
                    of beauty and brains, now languishing as
                    a wife and mother
Alfred   mid- to late forties, Rita's husband, a
                    once-promising writer, has just made a
                    life-changing realization about his career
                    and family
Asta   midtwenties, Rita's half-sister, still the
                    pretty young thing Rita once was
Wolfie   mid-teens, Alfred and Rita's adopted son,
                    native, was "special needs" for much of
                    his life, now trying to assert himself
Borghejm   fifties–sixties, female, native, a residen-
                    tial school survivor, and member of the
                    family who own Rita's leasehold
Old Woman   ageless, mythic (doubled with Borghejm
                    and an alter ego of sorts)

SETTING

ACT I: The kitchen and back garden of a family
                    cottage on native leasehold land north of
                    Deep Cove.
ACT II: A clearing in the woods.

TIME

Summer. The present.

ACT I

Dark woods. A hard BC rain falling. Sparse, haunting music: a drum, a voice.

Onstage an OLD WOMAN, *native, sits on a stump or log, hunched inside a traditional bark cape and spruce rain hat. She is perhaps the source of the music, perhaps not.*

Enter WOLFIE, *a native youth in his mid-teens, breathing heavily, drenched to the skin in his modern clothes. He blinks and squints at his surroundings. He finds the* OLD WOMAN *in the shadows of the forest.*

WOLFIE: Grampa? That you? Jordan?

The OLD WOMAN *ignores him.*

                    Hello? Is this it? Am I here?

The OLD WOMAN *pulls a bottle of hard liquor from her cape and takes a drink.*

OLD WOMAN: Who in the fuck you callin' Grampa, boy?

WOLFIE: I'm sorry. I lost my glasses.

OLD WOMAN: You're a retard is what it amounts to.

WOLFIE: No. No, I . . .

The OLD WOMAN *laughs at him.*

                    I'll be on my way.

OLD WOMAN: Where do you think you're going?

WOLFIE: I'm looking for the Lost Island.

The OLD WOMAN *laughs, harder than before.*

OLD WOMAN: Only one lost is you, you retard.

WOLFIE: Stop calling me that! I . . . I had cerebral hypoxia when I was a baby—

OLD WOMAN: Oh? Is that your excuse?

WOLFIE: My brain didn't get enough oxygen, okay?

OLD WOMAN: Cuz your mama was a drunken whore. Fuckin' heroin addict.

WOLFIE: NO!

OLD WOMAN: What do you know, boy? For all you know she stuffed you in a garbage bag and left you out back of St. Paul's. Out by the dumpsters.

WOLFIE: No she never. She put me up for adoption. She was young, that's all. She couldn't take care of me and she put me up for adoption.

OLD WOMAN: Why you so retarded then? Were you a preemie? Cord wrap around your neck when you was born?

WOLFIE: No.

OLD WOMAN: So what happened to ya?

WOLFIE: I . . . I . . .

WOLFIE is at a loss. The OLD WOMAN laughs.

OLD WOMAN: Just another dumb Indian.

WOLFIE: Fuck you. I'm going.

OLD WOMAN: Ain't gonna find nuthin'. Lost Island? It's lost, ain't it? What the hell you think you're gonna find there?

WOLFIE: Our courage. Our strength. Our wisdom. It's there. My grampa knew it.

OLD WOMAN: Your grampa? Your adopted grampa? Ol' Erik the Red? He was a white man, moron.

WOLFIE: He was good. He loved this land. He was a giant among men. A warrior. And so was Jordan. Jordan was a warrior and he was looking for the Lost Island, too. What he was saying is, it's time for us Indian men to warrior up. And I'm gonna follow him. I'm gonna find the Island, and we're gonna rise up and be strong and live righteously, and . . . and . . . we're gonna . . . we're gonna—

OLD WOMAN: *(mocking)* We're gonna . . . we're gonna . . .

WOLFIE: We're gonna rock the world, you old hag! I'll show you! I'll show you!

The OLD WOMAN laughs.

OLD WOMAN: *(stereotypical elder voice)* "Yes," said my old tillicum. "We Indians have lost many things . . . We may travel many days up the mountain trails, and look in the silent places for them. They are not

5

there. We may paddle many moons on the sea, but our canoes will never enter the channel that leads to the yesterdays of the Indian people. These things are lost, just like 'The Island of the North Arm.' "

WOLFIE: That's it. So you do know.

OLD WOMAN: Fuckin' fairy tale.

WOLFIE: No it isn't, it's a myth, an ancient *myth*. Myths are true. There's a difference—

OLD WOMAN: Myth as in fiction, boy. Myth as in the pretty little lies white people tell to gussy up the mud and shit we all came from.

WOLFIE: Shut up. Who are you? You're a witch. I'm not listening to you.

OLD WOMAN: A witch, eh? Since we're talkin' myths maybe I'm Raven. Maybe I'm Great Spirit herself. *(gestures to the woods all around)* Well here you go, boy. Here's your Lost Island. Your Happy Huntin' Grounds.

The OLD WOMAN stands with a decrepit blanket. She indicates their surroundings.

This is all there is, boy. Sky full of cold hard rain, woods full of smallpox and TB. So come on now. Come lie with me. I'm a beautiful young maiden, can'tcha see? Got a blanket for ya, right here.

She closes in on WOLFIE with the blanket.

WOLFIE: No . . . No . . . ! Get away from me! Get away! Mom! Dad—!

Darkness closes around them. The music and rain crescendo then cross-fade to the sound of a television newscast.

REPORTER: *(voice only)* —reports of an individual on the bridge deck. Whether this is a distraught person or a demonstrator of some sort, we simply don't know—

ANCHOR: *(voice only)* —and we're getting live images now from our Chopper One, Eye-in-the-Sky. Police cruisers mid-span, officers—it appears—with weapons drawn. Again these are live images. A disturbance in progress on the Ironworkers Memorial . . .

TV sounds continue in the background as lights come up on the back kitchen of a rustic cottage in the woods. Large windows and French doors overlook a garden with the waters of Indian Arm beyond. DIY home renovation and cleaning supplies are scattered here and there.

RITA stands at the windows with a glass of wine. Beside her on the counter is a three-litre box of wine. She stands there drinking, contemplating a strip of blue painter's tape in her hand. We hear a knock and the front door opening.

ASTA: *(off)* Hello! Rita? Wolfie? Ding-dong!

RITA sticks the tape on a memo board, downs her wine, dries the glass with a dishcloth, and puts it with some unused ones on a drink cart.

RITA: In here, sweetie!

She makes a show of working on the window frame.

ASTA: *(off)* Wow. *Wow.*

The TV turns off. ASTA *breezes in. She's a standard West Coast pretty young thing dressed and accessorized for maximum cuteness. She is waving a manila envelope.*

Rita! Hey!

The sisters hug and kiss.

RITA: Hey . . . Asta. Feels like ages.

ASTA: I know. Look at this place.

RITA: Oh, just little projects here and there.

ASTA: Listen to you, Martha Stewart.

                 (re: window frame) Should you even be doing that?

RITA: Doing what?

ASTA: You're stripping the patina.

RITA: It's fifty years of man-grime. The patina!

ASTA: It's Papa's man-grime. It's supposed to smell like smoke and pork rinds in here.

RITA: Well god forbid I should clean and make it feel homey.

ASTA: Whattaya gonna live here or what? It's like you're moving in.

RITA: I just want to be comfortable when I *am* here. Don't you? No point pretending we're in the wilderness anymore.

ASTA: Not when you're kicking back in front of the flat screen. It was on by the way. And

your porch lights. Don't turn into your
mum, okay—you're too young. I didn't
just say that.

RITA is not amused.

I'm kidding. It does feel homey. It's nice,
Rita. It's . . . welcoming.

RITA: It is, right? That's all I'm going for. So
welcome. Let's have a drink.

*RITA starts pouring wine but ASTA pours a glass of water
from a Brita pitcher.*

ASTA: You don't need these things, you know.
Our tap water's world-class.

RITA: Really?

ASTA: Sorry. *Sorry.* Where's my nephew? I had
this crazy dream.

RITA: He's outside with Alfred.

ASTA: Shut up—Freddie's back? This whole
thing's starting to feel like a premonition or something. *(re: manila envelope)*
First I find these papers, and then I have
this dream with Freddie and Wolfie, and
then, okay, you would not believe my
adventure just now getting this to you.

RITA: How did you manage? The bridge is
shut down.

ASTA: Yeah there's a jumper or something. So
you *were* watching TV. Anyway, I find
this stuff yesterday and then last night
I have this intense dream. Alfred and

I are at Sunny Hill, right, for Wolfie's therapy—

RITA: Why would you dream about that? We haven't been there in years.

ASTA: It's a dream.

RITA: Just cut to the chase.

ASTA: It's not about his therapy or anything.

RITA: Yeah but other people's dreams. Kinda had to be there.

ASTA: Rain on my parade.

RITA: Just show me the papers, Asta.

ASTA: No, I'm telling the story. Geez. Anyway, I wake up and I'm like gotta go show Rita. And I'm halfway down Barnet when the news lady says police incident, bridge closed, blah-de-blah. Well, I'm not gonna drive all the way to Lion's Gate and back through North Van. So I turn around and on a lark I pull into Reed Point. And as soon as I get out of my car I see this rich guy by his boathouse, totally checking me out, right, like looking at me sideways through his sunglasses? So I'm like, *(flirty)* "Hey . . . is there any chance you're going up the Arm anytime soon? I could really use a ride." And he's like, "Oh geez, I am now, sweetheart. But my wife's gonna kill me." And I'm like, "Who's telling?" And he points across the water to Ioco and he goes, "She's got binoculars." For real. "She's got binoculars!"

RITA: You hitched here on a boat with a perfect stranger.

ASTA: A yacht. Hilarious. Probably cost him eighty bucks in diesel. And one minute he's like Captain Suave, and the next minute he's all married and feeling guilty. I should've done like sun salutations on his deck. Given him a show.

RITA: Is this how you girls behave now?

ASTA: Everything I do I learned from you, big sister. Like you didn't flaunt it back in your day.

RITA: Back in my—? I still got it, okay? And when you got it, you don't need to flaunt. Remind me to tell you what happened at Honey's the other day.

ASTA: What, tell me now.

RITA: No, no, you corrupt a married man and commandeer a yacht to bring me these documents, I wanna see, I wanna see what you got.

ASTA: Okay but I'm hearing about Honey's. It better be good.

RITA: Oh it's good.

RITA holds out her hand. ASTA hands her the manila envelope. RITA pulls out an old soiled document.

         Okay. And this, Asta? This is good?

ASTA: It's Papa's lease. That's what it looks like anyway.

*RITA squints at the paper from a distance as if she has
reading glasses on, which she doesn't.*

Whattaya need glasses now?

RITA: No I do not need glasses. And you're
gonna be my age one day. What I do need
is a law degree. "The undersigned less-*or*
has let and demised unto the undersigned less-*ee* . . ." Who wrote this? I
mean, we're talking Papa in the bush
with a bunch of Indians. I was thinking
a shot of whisky and an IOU scrawled on
a pack of smokes. I didn't just say *that*
either.

ASTA: Well we're even now.

RITA: Uh, no, you made a crack about Martha
Stewart and "back in my day," the glasses,
and the whole yacht incident counts for
three. It's like six to one now and you've
only been here five minutes.

ASTA: Oh so we're keeping score.

RITA: Somebody's always keeping score. Age,
weight, carbon footprint. *Sins.* You believe
in karma. That's keeping score. *(pause)*
Let's get Alfred to read this. *(calls out the
window)* Freddie!

ASTA: When did he get back? I thought his
retreat thingy went for another two
weeks.

RITA: Yeah, no, he came back last night.

ASTA: Just like that?

RITA:	He texted from the airport. "On my way." You know. Mr. Communicative.
ASTA:	Did something happen?
RITA:	Like what? I dunno. He didn't say anything.
ASTA:	Well, good for you. Good to have your man back.
RITA:	It is. It's been a hard summer. Trying to get this place cleaned up, driving to Home Depot every three hours, *the money* . . . And Wolfie, god, you would not believe, talking back, testing how far he can push me . . .
ASTA:	Maybe you just need to give him some rope.
RITA:	As if. He's an asshole as it is. My child. How did this happen?
ASTA:	Just don't be on him so much, Rita, he's a pretty normal kid now.
RITA:	Normal? You don't know the half of it. And on top of everything else . . .

She picks up the papers.

Thank god for this.

ASTA:	Why, what's been happening?
RITA:	How long did Papa live here? Since the fifties. And in all that time what did the natives ever do with this land? Nothing. He's dead three months and now all of a sudden there's a dock, some sort of longhouse or something, and there's

this woman from the family, this *Mouse Woman* coming around all the time—

ASTA: Mouse Woman?

RITA: That's what Wolfie and I call her. She's literally like a mouse. Her hair, her clothes, the way she skulks around. And she's always bringing these gangs of native kids around now, having meetings, pow-wows, or whatever . . .

ASTA: And she's from the family?

RITA: I assume. After Byron died there was . . . Jared? Couple others. Then the two girls. She must be the elder now.

ASTA: Did you guys talk or what?

RITA: She came by one day, said she wanted to talk about the land. I'm like, lady, my father just died and my husband is away. Can we at least wait until he gets back? "Take your time," she says. "I ain't going nowhere." And pretty much every day now I see her creeping around. I just get this feeling from her, you know? Wolfie, too.

ASTA: She wants us gone?

RITA: Either that or force us to pay fair market. It's so cutthroat, so heartless. To think what Papa did for her family. I mean he saved them from that school. He literally saved their lives.

ASTA: I'm so sorry, Rita. *(re: papers)* This will help, right?

RITA:	It fucking better. And where have you been all summer? I could've really used your company. You haven't visited since Alfred left.
ASTA:	I was in Nicaragua with my mom, you know that.
RITA:	You've been back for weeks.
ASTA:	I thought you wanted some space to remember Papa. It's what you said. You were looking forward to spending the summer up here with Wolfie, just the two of you.
RITA:	We missed you.
ASTA:	I missed you guys. And so did Freddie, I bet. Maybe that's why he came back early. He missed you. Missed a little somethin-somethin.
RITA:	Mm.
ASTA:	Yeah? Fun night?

RITA abruptly calls out the French doors.

RITA:	Alfred! Wolfie! *(pause)* Must've gone for a walk.
ASTA:	So he got his writing done or what?
RITA:	Asta, I dunno, okay? He got in late and . . . Like he tells me anything. It's actually good you're here because he'll probably tell *you* and then *I'll* know. *(returns to document)* Where did you find this anyway?

ASTA: PoCo. My mom's storage locker. The documentary guy who's obsessed with Papa, he's constantly asking me for old photos and shit. So yesterday I go to the locker—literally just so I can tell the guy I looked—and the first box I touch— voila. Oh, and you gotta see these . . .

She digs a few more items from the manila envelope: some old photos.

This is like right here before he built the original cabin. That's the boulder right there in the garden.

RITA: Oh my god. *Oh my god. (pause)* Fuck, he was handsome.

ASTA: I know, right.

RITA: Look at his chest. It's like a barrel. They don't make men like that anymore.

ASTA: No they don't.

RITA: Imagine how big his heart was in a chest like that.

ASTA: It was so big, it blew up.

RITA flips to another photo.

RITA: Holy shit, that's Chief Dan George.

ASTA: Where?

RITA: In the back there with the children. That's Chief Dan George. What men they were. They were legends. Movie stars . . .

ASTA:	Papa should have been a movie star.
RITA:	He was to these kids—Erik the Red they called him. And oh my god, Asta, once when I babysat you—you were like five— we were watching some Western, Paul Newman, you know, and Sundance, and you said, "Rita, is there one of these with Papa in it? Next time let's watch one with Papa." So when he got home I told him and—god I'm gonna cry—he laughed and got all shy like he would do, and we went in to look at you sleeping and . . . he just started weeping. Like tears, weeping . . .
ASTA:	Awww. He'd cry on a dime. He liked it or something.
RITA:	He did. He was just a big teddy bear.

They look at the pictures and get teary themselves, remembering. RITA *hugs* ASTA *and covers her face with kisses.*

> You know what, baby girl? I think you saved us. You saved this cabin. Thank you. Thank you thank you thank you . . .

RITA *gets a hold of herself after a beat and goes for the drink cart.*

> Come on. Have a drink with me.

ASTA:	I'm good with water.
RITA:	Half a glass. We're celebrating.

She refills her glass, pours ASTA *one as well.*

ASTA:	Honestly I'm trying not to. That's all I did with Mum.

RITA: Wet your beak, don't make me drink alone.

ASTA: I don't want to get fat.

RITA: Shut up.

ASTA: Well I don't.

RITA: It's a glass of wine. A hundred calories.

ASTA: Wow, you *are* keeping score.

RITA: Anyway, how are you and your perky little ass gonna get fat doing Bikram five times a week?

ASTA: Pfft. I quit.

RITA: No.

ASTA: Yoga's done. The pants, the sex scandals. It's like this ancient and beautiful spiritual practice turned into Starbucks for your soul. I'm just gonna exercise. Pilates or Tabata or whatever. If I need to be spiritual I'll sit on a rock and look at the water. *(pause)* What?

RITA: I'm surprised.

ASTA: Well you know what? I divested, too.

RITA: Divested?

ASTA: All my lulu stock.

RITA: Sweetie, when your mother buys you a thousand shares of the IPO and you sell for, what, a four-bagger? More? That's not divesting, that's a killing. Divesting is a political or ethic—

ASTA: Yeah, I get it, Rita. I didn't bring down apartheid or save some valley on the Island from being clear-cut or whatever you think makes your generation superior to mine, okay? But since you're keeping score, this is my little statement in my little life.

RITA: Wraa-wraa-wraa. You don't have to get mad. I'm just telling you what the word means—

ASTA: I get it.

RITA: Well good for you. What are you gonna do with all that money?

ASTA: I dunno. Live off it? Mum wants me down in Nicaragua with her for a while.

RITA: What is going on with her?

ASTA: Oh her and her organic farmer guy, they're all into gold and Armageddon. They're like the whole system is not only a house of cards, it's upside down, so one breath, one butterfly flapping, and it's done.

RITA: And Nicaragua is safe because . . . ?

ASTA: They're in this gated "eco" expat utopia. It's like the hippie commune they *might* have lived in for two weeks when they were eighteen, only now they're all rich baby boomers with natives doing the grunt work. And every week they drive to the big box in Managua and load up on pallets of American food. The world will end and they'll be out by the infinity pool eating quinoa salad with little tins of smoked oysters.

RITA: I can just see her now lounging in her muumuu. Shoot me if you ever see me wearing one.

ASTA: Ditto. How's *your* mum?

RITA: Oh, you know. Good days, bad days. Mostly bad.

ASTA: Does she recognize you?

RITA: I like to think so. On some level.

ASTA: That must be so hard for you.

RITA: I said goodbye a long time ago. I'm the matriarch now. I command you to drink.

ASTA: Long live Queen Rita.

RITA: Oh. You *are* psychic.

ASTA: What.

RITA: Queen Rita. My Honey's story.

ASTA: Someone called you Queen Rita?

RITA: No. Do you know what a MILF is?

ASTA: Yeah, duh.

RITA: I don't keep up with these things so—

ASTA:	So, what, some horny teenagers called you a MILF?
RITA:	No, they were your age.
ASTA:	And you took it as a compliment?
RITA:	Do you want to hear the story or not?
ASTA:	I'm worried now.
RITA:	Shut up. You and your leering geriatric boat captain.
ASTA:	My story was cute. I'm worried yours is gonna be gross.
RITA:	*"My story was cute."* Forget it. I'm not competing with you and your twentysomething-ness.

She downs her glass. Finito.

ASTA:	Rita. Don't do that. Go. *Go.* I want to hear it.
RITA:	Drink, I said.

RITA refills her glass. ASTA drinks.

	My story is not gross. It's actually . . . well . . . there's an intrigue. A certain *frisson* if you know what I mean.
ASTA:	Oh.
RITA:	I was in the Cove to pick up some things. Wolfie stayed home—I let him do that by the way—and it starts pissing down rain, so I pop in to Honey's.

ASTA:	For a doughnut.
RITA:	They're too big for me.
ASTA:	Liar.
RITA:	I just wanted to get out of the rain and sit with a coffee. Well. There's four construction workers along the side. Young men. And as soon as I walk in, I hear these comments.
ASTA:	MILF.
RITA:	Cougar. You know. And yes I was wearing my yoga pants, but maybe I'll get rid of them now in light of your political stance—
ASTA:	Anyway.
RITA:	Anyway, they're not even trying to be discreet. Everyone can hear them. And there's two menopausal old cows by the window looking at me like it's my fault. Well, I decide I'm not going to sit in here and take this. So I get a macchiato to go, and of course the stupid lids, there's three sizes, none of them fit, I jam one on, I'm rushing because I feel like people are watching me, and when I pick up my coffee it spills everywhere. And I just cry out, "Unh!" like that. "Unh!" Next thing you know, the boys are busting a gut and I hear: "Now we don't have to guess what she sounds like either." Grown men. And the women by the window are giving *me* the stink eye. So I just say to the room basically, "Thanks for that," and I chuck the coffee in the garbage and leave.

ASTA: Good for you.

RITA: So now I'm in the car, about to pull out, and here comes one of the guys and . . . *oh my god* . . . Asta. I know he probably is an actual construction worker, but he's sauntering over like Magic fucking Mike. I mean he's got the perfect stubble and the bleached smile which you know he practises, and he's oozing this attitude, like, "God my dick is beautiful! And my balls are so smooth you can see yourself!" You know?

ASTA: Nice visuals, Rita.

RITA: Now here comes the tingly intriguing part. He walks up to the car and he says, "Hey, I know me and the crew were being rude and I just want to apologize." And he presents me with a macchiato with a flower design in the foam. And as I take it, I see he's taped his phone number to the cup with a piece of blue painter's tape. "For you," he says. "Cuz in my eyes, you're fable. A totally fable queen." *A totally fable queen.* Ungrammatical, yes, but there's a certain *je ne sais quoi*, don't you think? A chivalrous charm?

ASTA: Uh . . . Dude's got a pair, I'll give him that. What's his name?

RITA: No name. Just the number.

ASTA: Did you call him.

RITA: No.

ASTA: Are you gonna?

RITA: Are you crazy? I threw it away.

ASTA: You didn't. You said yourself it's intriguing.

RITA: Narcissists are not intriguing, Asta. Only to themselves. What is intriguing to me is this "fable queen" comment. Does it mean anything?

ASTA: Like what?

RITA: Like is it lingo for something. MILF. Cougar. Fable queen?

ASTA: I dunno. It's a mystery. *(re: memo board)* Anyway if you're gonna keep that piece of tape around you should probably hide it before Freddie sees it.

RITA: Oh. I thought I tossed that. I'm just keeping it for a laugh.

Sounds of horseplay off. WOLFIE enters through the French doors. He's a native boy in his mid-teens, with thick heavy-framed glasses but dressed in something high on style points: e.g., English Premiere League jersey and brand name athletic shoes. Right behind him is ALFRED in a rumpled dress shirt and jeans.

WOLFIE: Oh hey, Auntie.

ASTA: Wolfie! What kind of a greeting is that? Come here, you.

She hugs him, covers him with kisses, tousles his hair, etc.

WOLFIE: Auntie!

He squirms away but clearly enjoys her attentions.

Do you like my new clothes? Dad got them for me and he's signing me up for soccer and swimming. And guess what else—Aboriginal camp!

RITA: Oh really?

ASTA: Good for you, dude. And sick threads. You're turning into quite the hottie.

WOLFIE: Nah, whatever.

ASTA: Auntie ain't gonna lie to you.

ALFRED: My turn.

ASTA: Hello, Freddie.

ALFRED: You're a sight for sore eyes.

They embrace, nothing improper, but RITA *doesn't like it.* ASTA *knows this.*

ASTA: Look at your handsome men, Rita.

RITA: But they only have eyes for you.

ASTA: Rita—

ALFRED: Nonsense—

WOLFIE: Auntie *is* a looker.

ASTA: Thanks, Wolfman. Not so bad yourself.

They canoodle playfully. It takes them a short distance away.

RITA: *(sotto)* Alfred. Aboriginal camp?

ALFRED: That kayak and wilderness camp out of Cates Park.

RITA: Kayak? He can't swim—

WOLFIE: *(overhears)* That's why I'm learning.

RITA: Wolfie, the reality is you still have a special needs assistant at school—

WOLFIE: But I don't actually need her, Mom.

RITA: What if you lose your glasses? You can barely—

WOLFIE: I'm not a baby—I'm almost sixteen! And I'm Indian. I *am* Indian, you know. You don't teach me anything. Who's gonna teach me now that Grampa's dead? In the old days I'd have gone on a vision quest and found my totem animal and be a warrior by now.

RITA: Sweetheart, it's not safe for you. When you're in unfamiliar surroundings—

WOLFIE: Just give me a chance for once. I'll show you. *I'll show you.*

He starts ululating like a Hollywood brave. A beat later he stops abruptly and plops himself down at the counter.

Can I have some chocolate milk?

RITA: No.

RITA plonks a glass and the Brita pitcher in front of him.

WOLFIE: Water's good. *(sarcastically polite)* Thank you, Mother.

ALFRED: *(to ASTA)* So how was Nicaragua?

ASTA: Oh . . . you know, beautiful and sad. Every time you're on a gorgeous beach there's a billboard in the background showing you what it will look like all glitzed up with condos.

RITA: Imagine if they did that with people. Imagine if there was a billboard behind Asta right now showing what she'll look like when she's middle-aged and married to some Land Rover liberal.

ASTA: Why I'll look just like you, Rita.

ALFRED: Hey! What does that make me?

WOLFIE: Land Rover liberal, Land Rover liberal, Land Rover liberal. Say it three times fast.

ALFRED: Good one, Wolf. *(to ASTA)* Did I ever tell you my Nicaragua story? My truck and the Sandinistas?

ASTA: You drove your truck to Nicaragua?

ALFRED: No, but that's the thing.

WOLFIE: What are Sandinistas?

ALFRED: Well when I was in college, Wolf, there were people in Nicaragua called Sandinistas who felt the country should belong to everyone, not just the rich—

RITA: Spare us the history lesson, Alfred. Tell them about your dream, Asta. *(to WOLFIE and ALFRED)* She dreamt you were at Sunny Hill.

The mention of Sunny Hill sours the mood.

WOLFIE: Oh.

ALFRED: Huh.

WOLFIE: Was it a nightmare, Auntie?

ASTA: No. Um . . .

RITA: It was like a premonition, isn't that right?

ASTA: Yeah . . . It was weird . . . *(pause)* You know
              what? I'm totally drawing a blank now.

WOLFIE: When you have a premonition does that
              mean you can see the future? Like what's
              gonna happen to you?

ALFRED: No, no, Wolf, it's just a feeling that some-
              thing might happen.

WOLFIE: I had a dream like that last night, too.
              It was scary.

ALFRED: Yeah, I thought I heard you calling out
              in your sleep.

*WOLFIE and ASTA exchange a look. An expectation that one
or the other will speak, but it passes.*

              Anyway, Sandinistas—

RITA: Spare us, I said. What happened on your
              retreat? What have you been working on
              all summer?

ASTA: Yes, what have you been scribbling away
              at? Whatever it is, you look refreshed.

ALFRED: I feel refreshed. *Renewed.*

RITA: You were dead tired last night.

ALFRED: And now I feel renewed.

WOLFIE: Auntie, want to see my new soccer ball?

ASTA: In a minute, Wolf. *(to ALFRED)* So I guess
               your writing went well?

ALFRED: I didn't write a single word actually.

RITA: What?

WOLFIE: You gotta see it, Auntie, it's an
               official FIFA—

RITA: Wolf, grown-ups are talking. You were
               gone six weeks, Alfred.

ALFRED: I did a lot of thinking. I made some
               realizations.

RITA: Do tell.

ALFRED: Oh. I don't want to bore you.

WOLFIE: Dad's gonna home-school me from now on.

RITA: What?

ALFRED: Let's talk about it over dinner, okay? *(to
               ASTA)* You're staying, right?

ASTA: Um . . .

WOLFIE: Please, Auntie? I want to show you my
               new road in *Minecraft.*

RITA: Wolfie! *(pause)* Alfred?

ALFRED: We don't have to get into this right now. I
             can tell you're getting a little upset. And
             it's no criticism of you, Rita. You've done
             a great job. I just think it's time I was
             more involved. Let's talk about it later.

RITA: Well. Sounds like I'm going for groceries.

ASTA: Rita, don't trouble yourself.

RITA: No, no, I need some air. You have no way
             of getting home anyway. You arrived on
             a boat.

*RITA makes a show of gathering up shopping bags, getting
a list together, etc.*

ALFRED: A boat? Where did you put in?

ASTA: That new dock the band built.

ALFRED: Why'd you come on a boat?

ASTA: There's a jumper on the bridge.

ALFRED: Really?

*ALFRED whips out his smartphone, starts googling. RITA
throws a cupboard open, pokes around with annoyance.*

             Rita, stop. We'll all go out to eat.

She ignores him. ALFRED reports what he found:

             Huh. Now they're saying native activ-
             ist . . . Pipeline . . . Idle No More . . . Who
             knows. Maybe he's from the band here.

ASTA: Well right on, then. Good for him.

ALFRED: Yeah. Then again, goombah made you take a boat.

ASTA: Goombah? What is he, Sicilian?

ALFRED: Well not to be racist but they're like the frikkin' mob sometimes, aren't they? All their demands and protests. Which I totally get but—

ASTA: Freddie. I'm surprised at you.

WOLFIE: Whenever Dad says "not to be racist" he kinda is, and whenever he says "frikkin'" he actually means the F-word.

RITA: Wolfgang! Do you need to go to your room?

WOLFIE: I'm just sayin'. Right, Dad?

ALFRED: You're right. *(to ASTA)* You're right. I was being flip. My bad.

WOLFIE: *(to RITA)* See? Boom! Go shopping.

RITA: That is enough! *(to ALFRED and ASTA)* Some help here?

ALFRED: Sometimes you have to keep your observations to yourself, Wolf.

WOLFIE: Why?

RITA: Because you're being rude and insolent and you're driving me up the wall— that's why!

ASTA: You were really disrespectful, Wolfie. Not cool.

WOLFIE: Okay, sorry.

ASTA: Come on, let's leave your mom and dad alone.

ALFRED: You don't have to do that.

WOLFIE: Wanna hang in my room?

ASTA: Sure—

RITA: No, she does not. *(to WOLFIE)* Go outside.

WOLFIE: I just was outside. I was outside all day with Dad.

ASTA: Hey, go get your soccer ball. Auntie's got some moves.

WOLFIE: Okay. Awesome. *(to RITA)* Happy?

WOLFIE exits. ASTA heads for the French doors.

RITA: *(to ASTA)* I want a word with you. *(to ALFRED)* Asta found Papa's lease papers. Have a look, please.

RITA stalks past ASTA into the garden. ASTA exchanges a look with ALFRED, then follows RITA out. ALFRED turns his attention to the papers.

In the garden:

How 'bout you turn it down a notch.

ASTA: Turn what down?

RITA:	Put on a shirt or a sweater or something.
ASTA:	Says Rita the *fable queen*.
RITA:	Oh, so you do know what it means.
ASTA:	No, I just think it's ridiculous how proud you are that you got hit on by a moron with a hard hat.
RITA:	You're the one getting your jollies making Wolfie spaz out.
ASTA:	I'm just teasing him.
RITA:	Exactly. It's confusing to him.
ASTA:	Rita. I'm his auntie.
RITA:	And I'm his mother.
ASTA:	Well stop sss-mothering him.
RITA:	Excuse me?
ASTA:	He's a pretty normal kid now.
RITA:	If you only knew what I'm going through with him—
ASTA:	Like what.
RITA:	Like . . . puberty. Women. It's gross. And then this whole identity thing.
ASTA:	He's a teenage boy. Whattaya gonna do? Freddie should have a talk with him if you're worried.
RITA:	Freddie. Like he's helping.

ASTA: Soccer, camp, some cool clothes. And Freddie wants to be more involved. That's great. It's all normal stuff—

WOLFIE arrives with the soccer ball.

RITA: Stop saying it's normal!

WOLFIE: Ready, Auntie?

ASTA: Yeah, let's go.

She makes a point of putting her arm through WOLFIE's. He likes it. They exit through the garden. RITA storms into the kitchen and pours herself another glass of wine. ALFRED snuggles up behind her, tries to make nice.

ALFRED: Hey. I'm glad we're all together, aren't you? First time all summer. I can't believe Asta took a boat here.

RITA: Oh how things have changed, Alfred. When you married me a boat or a half-hour hike through blackflies was the only way you could get here. And you loved it. "We, who had the gold and the green forests." You sat in this very kitchen and wrote your GG masterpiece, pretending you were Malcolm Lowry.

ALFRED: I still pretend I'm Malcolm Lowry. Only now there's a road and Wi-Fi and municipal water. And I like it that way.

He turns to the papers.

You want to talk about this?

RITA: "Oh let's talk over dinner."

ALFRED: I think we should consider the implications.

RITA: The implications are we have leasehold
            paper and there are laws about eviction,
            about how much you can increase rent.
            The courts settled this years ago in the
            Southlands with the Musqueam. End of
            discussion.

ALFRED: I think this is different.

RITA: No it isn't.

ALFRED: We're on a reserve. Your father was
            allowed to live here because of the per-
            sonal relationships he had.

RITA: But it turns out we also have papers. A
            contract.

ALFRED: Did you even read this?

RITA: The point is they can't just boot us off
            the land now or raise the rent 10,000
            per cent or whatever the hell they want
            to do.

ALFRED: We don't really know what they want
            to do. Do we? What's been going on this
            summer? Besides you sinking all our
            money into—

RITA: Ohhh money! I'm not getting into this now.

ALFRED: You can't just ignore this, Rita—

RITA: I have to go shopping.

ALFRED: How much have you had to drink?

She starts off. He stops her.

RITA: Please.

ALFRED: Rita. Relax. Let's go out for dinner.

RITA: What, pizza? A&W?

ALFRED: We can feed Asta and Wolf some mac
                'n' cheese and you and I can go out
                somewhere nice. Talk about this. Talk
                about us.

RITA: That's the first semi-loving thing you've
                said to me since you got home.

ALFRED: . . .

RITA: I get your three-word text from the air-
                port, Alfred, and you know what I do? I
                go into a frenzy getting ready for you.
                I tidy up. I turn on the porch lights so
                you won't have to stumble around in
                the dark. And then I bathe. I shave and
                tweeze every stray hair from my skin.
                I put new sheets on the bed. I light
                candles. I put on the fucking girlie-girl
                lingerie that *you* like, and I lie here wait-
                ing for you. And you come home and it's
                like you're blind to anything I do.

He touches her tenderly.

ALFRED: Hey . . . *Hey* . . . I actually was kinda
                blind last night. I got this excruciating
                headache when the plane was—

A growl of frustration. RITA *tries to go.* ALFRED *grabs
her arm.*

Rita—

RITA: You had champagne, Alfred, but you touched it not.

She tries to pull away. He pulls her close, kisses her roughly, pushes his body into her.

ALFRED: Is this what you want? Huh?

RITA: Keep going. Let's see you start a fire you can't put out.

He gropes at her, puts his mouth on her. She starts to reciprocate, then pushes him away.

RITA: You don't feel it.

ALFRED: For Chrissakes, Rita, we're not seventeen.

RITA: We're not anything anymore. We're parents. Whoop-de-do.

ALFRED: I said let's go out. Have a nice romantic dinner. And yes, that's what it takes because we *are* parents and Wolfie *is* a handful. I mean, he has been for much of his life. But things are going to change, sweetheart. Look at how much he's come along just this summer. The light in his eyes, the confidence—

RITA: There. *There.* What was that?

ALFRED: What.

RITA: Right there, when you started talking about him. Your whole being was exuding your tenderness and love for him.

ALFRED: He's my son.

RITA: You do not ever—*ever*—look at me or speak to me with the same affection.

ALFRED: Of course I do.

RITA: "Of course I do." No, Alfred, you only have so much human feeling to go around. For years you put it into your work. And now? My papa's dead less than two months and off you go—

ALFRED: I came back early—

RITA: —you don't write a word—

ALFRED: —I came back early for you—

RITA: —and you're all full of love, aren't you? For pretty little Asta. *(bitterly)* For Wolfie. How I wish sometimes we'd never . . .

ALFRED: Oh? Never what?

RITA: I wish sometimes this dull, grey existence of ours would just . . . *explode*. I wish a landslide of screaming passion would come down the mountain and wash us out into the Arm. We'd float out there in the cabin, like it was an ark, just you and me. We'd lie in bed all day and night like we used to. Before we were married. Before Wolfie. Before . . .

ALFRED: One reckless, selfish moment of—

RITA: Don't! Don't think about that. Think about what we had. In the beginning. How beautiful we were together. And in love. We'd read to each other, we'd laugh and cry over poetry, we'd dream about changing the world.

ALFRED: Everybody does that, Rita. When they're young. When they have nothing to lose.

RITA: No they don't! Only we did! And I ache for it!

Silence. ALFRED *tries to be warm.*

ALFRED: Rita. My love. We did change the world. We still are. We adopted a native boy. We made a family with him. We gave him a world of opportunity. It's not glamorous, it's not sexy, but it's beautiful. And it is what we dreamed. Let's celebrate that. Let's get dressed up, go somewhere romantic, make a real date of it. And let's talk. Not about the past, about the future. Our future, Wolfie, this property—

RITA: I want to have sex.

ALFRED: We will.

RITA: Right now.

ALFRED: . . .

RITA: *Right now.* I don't want to hear about Wolfie and Asta coming back or some bullshit headache. I want you to fuck me like you mean it. You're my husband. I'm hot. It's been six weeks.

ALFRED: . . .

RITA: I'm dying. Why aren't you? Don't you want me? If you don't want me so help me god I don't know what I'll do. I'll give myself away. I'll throw myself at someone. Someone who wants me.

ALFRED: Oh yeah? Who?

RITA: There's men everywhere. Young. Hard. I'm a fable queen in their eyes.

ALFRED: A what?

RITA grabs the blue tape from the memo board.

RITA: You see this? This phone number? He called me a "fable queen." I'll call him. I'll let him have me if you won't.

ALFRED: Gimme that.

He takes the tape, crumples it, tosses it in the corner.

I want you. I do.

RITA: Prove it.

He embraces her, touches her. They slowly build up some arousal.

That's it. That's what I want.

A knock at the front door.

ALFRED: . . .

RITA: Fuck! Don't get it.

ALFRED: Who is it?

RITA: *Don't.*

She kisses him, rubs his crotch, etc., tries to get his attention back. Another knock.

BORGHEJM: *(offstage)* Hello?

RITA: Shhh. She's here about the lease.

ALFRED: We should talk to her.

RITA: I will rip your throat open.

ALFRED: . . .

RITA: Shit, she's coming around the back. Go! Go!

ALFRED: Rita—

RITA: Let's go! In the car!

She starts herding him out front. As they exit, RITA *kisses* ALFRED *hard.*

                 Fuck me in the car. On the side of the road.

ALFRED: . . .

RITA: *Fuck* me, do you understand?

ALFRED: Rita. Get a hold of yourself. This is—

She shoves him off and they exit. BORGHEJM *now appears in the garden. She's a native woman of about sixty dressed in nondescript outdoor attire.*

BORGHEJM: Hello? Anybody home?

The sound of car doors, the engine starting, the car driving off.

Oh, hey—

BORGHEJM goes after it, then realizes it's no use. She takes in the house and garden for a beat.

Been a long time, eh?

She starts talking to the ether.

You recognize me or what? It's me, Janice. It's all right—I wouldn't recognize myself. Remember the first time we laid eyes on each other? Byron brought you home and said, "This is Erik the Red, famous Viking!" Us kids were all so scared, me most of all, scared of your orange beard and your skin that looked like the sun burnt it off. Ten minutes later you had all six of us climbing all over you. And ten minutes after that we were all over that truck of yours. *Loki. Good ol' Loki.* We never laughed so hard, Erik. Not in those days.

You were like a wolf to us. Like the first wolf who brought our people a deer when we were starving. When we were all rotting up at that school, it got so we could hear Loki coming from a mile away. Oh what it meant to us to hear that sound, Erik, and to hear voices from home calling out as you drove back and forth, back and forth past the gate.

I'm sorry you lost your way. I did, too. Made it back though. And you're around here somewheres. I can feel you. The place looks good. 'Course I'll always have a soft spot for that first shack you and Byron built, all of us kids hiding out here like a bunch of squirrels, hiding until they tore that fucking school down . . .

Voices off.

WOLFIE: *(offstage)* Ow!

ASTA: *(offstage)* Okay, okay . . . Keep your head back.

BORGHEJM: *(to the ether)* Anyways . . . Good talkin' to ya . . .

WOLFIE and ASTA enter, tending to WOLFIE's nose which is bleeding.

WOLFIE: It's running down my throat. You coulda broke my glasses.

ASTA: You missed the header, dude, it's not my fault—

BORGHEJM: Hello.

ASTA: Oh. Can I help you?

BORGHEJM: I was looking for the Allmers. I think they just drove off.

ASTA: *(calls into the house)* Freddie! Rita? *(pause)* Went for groceries I guess. They should be back soon. *(re: bloody nose)* Let me just deal with this.

BORGHEJM: Sure thing.

ASTA: I'll get you a wet cloth, Wolf.

43

WOLFIE: No, Auntie. I'm coming with you.

ASTA: You stay with our guest. Be a gentleman.

WOLFIE: Auntie—

ASTA goes into the kitchen. WOLFIE is extremely uncomfortable being left alone. Long pause.

BORGHEJM: So you're the one they call Wolf, eh?

He stares off, seems to nod slightly.

                You know our people here, we're the Wolf
                Clan. We're children of the wolf.

He stares at his shoes, etc.

                Right over there by Belcarra, a mother
                wolf found a baby in the woods. She
                raised him like her own, raised him up
                to be a warrior, the first man of our—

WOLFIE: *(barely audible)* Grampa told me.

BORGHEJM: Say what?

WOLFIE: Grampa told me. He taught me about
                this land and about being an Indian.

BORGHEJM: Being native, right? Being *native.*

*WOLFIE shrugs. ASTA has finished preparing a wet cloth
but stays inside and listens through the window.*

                Your grampa was a great man. He and
                my brother were loggers together.

WOLFIE: I know. Grampa made roads, too.

BORGHEJM: Yes he did. He made the roads not taken if you know what I mean. Folks say he cut a trail all the way around the Arm.

WOLFIE: What do you know about it? Your brother help?

BORGHEJM: No. I think by that time your Grampa wanted to be by himself.

WOLFIE: You don't know then. It's a secret.

BORGHEJM: Well, it's more like a legend, eh? No secret he tried to do it. Did he finish is the question. And is it still there.

WOLFIE gets agitated, wipes his nose, gets blood over his hand. ASTA starts out with the cloth.

WOLFIE: It is still there. Why wouldn't it be?

BORGHEJM: He ruffled a lot of feathers. Cutting through park land, the watershed, private property—

WOLFIE: You don't know. That's not what he was doing. He was on a quest. Dad's writing a book about it.

This stops ASTA. She listens.

BORGHEJM: I hear your dad's a great man, too—great writer. I guess that makes you destined for great things as well.

WOLFIE: I had cerebral hypoxia when I was a baby. It changed my brain. It changed my retinal-cortical pathway.

BORGHEJM: You can say that again.

WOLFIE: In the old days they would've seen that I had special vision and they would've made me the seer of the tribe. Grampa told me so.

BORGHEJM: Could be you're a seer now.

WOLFIE: In *Minecraft* I found a jungle fortress and built a road to it. Three days walk from my house.

BORGHEJM: Maybe you'll be the one to find your grampa's trail. Follow it all the way around the Arm.

WOLFIE: That's not where it goes. *(secretive)* It goes to the Lost Island.

BORGHEJM: The Lost Island. Haven't heard that one in donkey's years.

WOLFIE: Pauline Johnson wrote it in a book. *Legends of Vancouver.* It was my grampa's favourite.

BORGHEJM: Yes, it was. Can you tell it?

WOLFIE: Sure I can. *(pause)* Long time ago, there was a medicine man. He was strong as a giant, and brave as a timber wolf. He saw a vision that there would be a great camp of pale-faces between the inlet and False Creek. A *premonition*, right? Of Vancouver. He saw the ports, the roads, the skyscrapers filled with white people. Thousands upon thousands of them. He saw the Indians become like them and lose all their strength and courage. He hated this vision and tried to kill it but it haunted him his whole life. So when

he was old and about to die, he pad-
dled up the Arm and hid all his power
and knowledge on an island so that his
people could reclaim it one day and be
strong and proud again. And ever since
then people have been looking for that
Lost Island. That was Grampa's quest.
And now Dad's gonna write a book about
it and it's gonna be epic!

*WOLFIE gets more blood on his hand. He starts wiping it
on his shirt.*

BORGHEJM: Hey, careful—

ASTA comes out with the cloth.

ASTA: Bravo, Wolf, great story. Here, clean your-
self up. *(to BORGHEJM)* Sorry to keep you.
I don't think we've ever met. I'm Asta.
Rita and I are sisters.

BORGHEJM: Oh, you're the younger daughter.

ASTA: Yes. And you're . . . from the family?

BORGHEJM: Janice. Borghejm. I'm the eldest still
living.

WOLFIE: My mom calls you Mouse Woman.

ASTA: Wolfie.

BORGHEJM: Hey, I'll take that as a compliment. *(to
WOLFIE)* Mouse Woman is a powerful
grandmother spirit. She makes things
right.

WOLFIE: That's not why my mom calls you—

ASTA: She makes thing right, Wolf. Good to know, yeah? *(to* BORGHEJM*)* Do you want me to pass anything along to Rita for you? Is it about the lease?

BORGHEJM: I did want to talk to her about that, yeah, but to tell you the truth I just came to borrow your phone.

ASTA: Oh, of course.

She passes BORGHEJM *her smartphone.* BORGHEJM *starts fiddling with it.*

BORGHEJM: So embarrassing. Drove up yesterday with a few of the youth—I counsel them, you know—the fresh air, sleeping all together in the longhouse, learning respect for themselves and for everything, it's good for them. *(to* WOLFIE*)* You should come join us. We talk about being native, being a warrior, being true to yourself in this day and age.

WOLFIE: My dad already signed me up for Aboriginal camp.

BORGHEJM: Well this one you don't have to sign up. Just come on by.

WOLFIE: Should I, Auntie? Think Mom will let me?

ASTA: I'll talk to her.

BORGHEJM: Anyways, I take the kids on a hike this morning, my nephew Jordan doesn't want to come. So we leave him, get back couple hours later, him and the van are gone. Took off with it somewhere. And I made all the kids leave their phones at home and mine was in the van, so . . .

WOLFIE: I know Jordan. I see him walking by our driveway. He talks to me all the time. He has a shirt that says "Warrior Up!" and his arms like bulge out of it. Me and Dad saw him this morning and when he saw us he said "Warrior Up!" *to me.*

BORGHEJM: That's him. You seen him walking around flexing his muscles, eh?

WOLFIE: He was in front of your longhouse. He was washing himself with smoke. Is he a warrior?

She holds up a finger, having finally succeeded in dialing a number.

(*to* ASTA) Auntie, isn't it a coincidence that we called her Mouse Woman, and she *is* the Mouse Woman?

ASTA: Wolfie, shush.

She tries to get WOLFIE *cleaned up as* BORGHEJM *talks.*

BORGHEJM: Oh, hey. It's Janice . . . Whoa whoa whoa—what are you talking about? What are you talking about? He's . . . *Jesus* . . . You sure it's him? And they're saying *what* now? They're calling him *what?* For fuck sakes—you gotta come get me, you gotta send somebody. Well he took it, right? He took the van. I'm up here at Inlailawatash with three other kids. You gotta send somebody to come get us and drive me to that bridge. Like

right now. Like right fucking now! Okay?
Okay . . .

She hangs up. Silence.

ASTA: He's on the bridge?

BORGHEJM: Do you have a car?

ASTA: No, I . . . You know what, I'll call Freddie
                 on his cell.

BORGHEJM: Could you? Could you please?

*The sound of a car pulling into the driveway, car doors
slamming.*

ASTA: That's them now. Come in. Come in . . .

*ASTA rushes in. WOLFIE follows her. BORGHEJM stays outside.
RITA stalks in opposite, ALFRED trailing some distance
behind. Things did not go well on the road. ASTA and
WOLFIE meet them in the kitchen.*

RITA: Why are you bleeding?

WOLFIE: Something bad is happening.

RITA: *(re: BORGHEJM)* What is she doing here?
                 (to ASTA) I thought I told you to put on
                 some clothes.

ASTA: Rita, stop. Take a breath. Freddie, she
                 needs your help—

RITA: *(heading for the garden)* Change clothes,
                 the both of you! *(to BORGHEJM)* What do
                 you want?

BORGHEJM: I . . . I need to borrow your car.

RITA: *Borrow my car?*

ALFRED: *(arriving in the garden)* What can I do for you?

BORGHEJM: Can I . . . can I speak to you, please . . .

RITA: Excuse me, no, you don't need to talk to him. My father is—

ASTA: Rita! It's not about that. Her nephew is on the bridge.

WOLFIE: He's a kid named Jordan, Mom, he's a warrior, and he took the van!

BORGHEJM: I need to talk to him. I . . . I'm hoping someone's on their way to get me, but if you have a car . . . I'm going a little crazy here.

ALFRED: Well, yeah, I guess—

RITA: No no no, what are you thinking? You won't get anywhere near the bridge. It's all shut down. *(to BORGHEJM)* This is a police matter. Your nephew needs to do as they say and be arrested.

ASTA: Rita!

BORGHEJM: Look, I'm scared for him, you understand? They're calling him some kind of radical or militant or something.

ASTA: We'll take you. We'll take you as close as we can. Won't we, Freddie?

ALFRED has been googling on his phone and reports what he has learned.

ALFRED:	He's barricaded himself inside a bus. They're saying he has a weapon.
RITA:	You see? You see—
BORGHEJM:	No . . . *No* . . . That's wrong. That's propaganda. He's a good kid. He's peaceful—
RITA:	You won't get within three miles of the bridge.
ASTA:	Freddie, is there anyone you know, anyone you can call?
ALFRED:	Like who?
BORGHEJM:	Anyone. On the news? Reporters?
ALFRED:	Well . . . I know some TV people but I don't know what they could do.
BORGHEJM:	They could stop calling him all these things. Stop making him out to be disturbed or violent or—
RITA:	Well what does he think he's doing up there?
BORGHEJM:	What is he doing? Are you fucking serious?

Silence.

Are you? *(pause)* Yeah he's on the bridge. It's reckless. It's stupid. I get it. But he's not some fucking terrorist, okay? He's my nephew. You don't think he has a reason? You don't think he has a hundred reasons?

BORGHEJM and RITA glare at each other.

ASTA: Freddie, let's just go or just call someone. Do something. Please. Let them know his aunt wants to talk to him.

ALFRED: Lemme see what I can do.

He thumbs at his phone and heads for the kitchen. WOLFIE follows.

Stay here, Wolf.

ALFRED exits through the kitchen to the front room. RITA calls after him:

RITA: Why are you getting involved? Didn't you call him a "goombah" a while ago?

ASTA: Rita. Really?

We hear the television come on, a wash of concerned, self-important voices.

BORGHEJM: I gotta get outta here.

RITA: Yes. Please do.

RITA wheels and stomps into the kitchen, beside herself. To WOLFIE as she goes:

For the last time, clean yourself up!

WOLFIE: No! It's my new shirt!

RITA sees the lease documents, grabs them, and storms back to BORGHEJM in the garden.

RITA: By the way, this is the lease agreement my father made with your family. Have a look at your convenience.

She leaves BORGHEJM with the papers and heads back inside. BORGHEJM is too shocked to speak.

(*to ASTA and WOLFIE*) I'm starting dinner. You two are having mac 'n' cheese.

She pours herself some wine, starts rummaging around for pots, etc. In the garden:

ASTA: Janice, I'm so sorry, I don't know why she's—

RITA: Do not apologize for me!

WOLFIE: Mom! Stop fighting with everyone! Stop! JUST STOP!

WOLFIE starts crying. ASTA tries to calm him down.

Something bad is happening . . . something bad is happening . . .

ASTA: Hey. Shhh. Everything's gonna be okay.

ALFRED comes back out to the garden.

ALFRED: You all right, Wolf?

WOLFIE: Mom is not herself today.

He starts crying harder and buries his face in ASTA's shoulder.

ALFRED: (*to BORGHEJM*) I called a CBC guy I know, I'm just getting voicemail. But listen, I just checked the news, it's a stalemate.

Your nephew's not in any immediate danger, okay? He's in the bus, the police are talking to him—that's the important thing—they're talking. I'm sure it's going to work out.

BORGHEJM: Dear god, I hope so.

ALFRED: Absolutely. Your band must have contacts, too, with the police, the city . . .

BORGHEJM: I suppose so. I have to get back. I got three other kids I'm supposed to be watching.

ALFRED: Well look . . . do you want me to drive you to the bridge? I'll take you as far as I can.

BORGHEJM: I gotta make sure these other kids are okay. And then if my ride's not here . . . *(hands him the papers)* We have this.

ALFRED: I figured.

BORGHEJM: Thanks anyways.

BORGHEJM exits through the garden. RITA comes out. Silence.

RITA: Wolfie, go inside.

WOLFIE: Make up your mind.

RITA: Do not start with me.

WOLFIE: Dad told me to stay outside.

RITA: And now I'm telling you to go inside. WOLFIE!

WOLFIE fumes with rage. Inexplicably, he angrily starts shouting the refrain from Simon and Garfunkel's "The Boxer."

WOLFIE: "Lie-la-lie! Lie-la-lie-lie-lie-la-lie . . . "

He storms inside but we see that he hovers within earshot.

ASTA: What was that?

ALFRED: Nothing. It's a joke.

ASTA: A joke?

RITA: All of a sudden everything's a joke around here and everybody's in on it but me, isn't that right, Alfred? *(re: lease papers)* You knew she had a copy?

ALFRED: That's usually how they do these things, Rita.

RITA: Don't talk to me like I'm stupid. If she has the lease papers why has that woman been on me all summer, treating me like some sort of squatter?

ALFRED: Are you sure that's what she's been doing? Because she seemed nice to me.

RITA: You're taking her side now? I am your wife.

ALFRED: This lease has a life estate provision. Do you know what that means? I don't want to talk to you like you're stupid but—

ASTA: Freddie. Just tell us.

ALFRED: This gave your father the right to enjoy this land—Lot 8, Inlailawatash Reserve 2A—*"for as long as he shall live."*

ASTA: So . . . now that he's dead . . .

RITA: So what? There are laws protecting surviving family from being evicted just because the leaseholder has died.

ALFRED: A spouse, dependant children, maybe. You're not a dependant child. Are you? And your mother divorced your father ages ago. Hell, your father hasn't lived here for years either. He'd just come in from the bush every few weeks to have a shower.

RITA: We can make a new lease then. A new agreement—

ALFRED: With who? We're on a reserve.

RITA: It's still Canada, isn't it? What do I need a visa now?

ALFRED: Now you're being ridiculous. I don't even think it's up to that woman and her family anymore. Without the personal relationships your father had, the goodwill with the band—

RITA: We'll cultivate our own relationships. You're an acclaimed author, Alfred. That woman asked for your help just now because of your name, your pull with the media. You could be like . . . *an artist-in-residence.* It would be prestigious for them to—

ALFRED: Rita, you're reaching for straws—

RITA: Because I'm drowning! *I'm drowning!* This is my home, my life, my childhood summers. My father carved this out of forest and rock. How do the natives have a greater claim to this? They don't even use this reserve, it just sits here. Vacant!

ASTA moves to comfort her. RITA turns on her.

Why aren't you upset? This is Papa's cabin!

ASTA: Maybe it's meant to be. Papa never believed in owning land or building anything permanent. Maybe this is how he wanted things.

RITA: He did not. He had principles. It would infuriate him, *infuriate him*, that these people have so much power over our lives, over land that we love, that we grew up on!

ASTA: I grew up in butt-fuck Burquitlam, Rita. For most of my life Papa was off the grid and off in the bush somewhere. I don't know that he wanted you or any of us to live on this land forever.

RITA: We are not the enemy here. We even have a son, a native boy who we adopted and cared for and—

She cuts herself off, struck with a revelation.

Oh my god. *Wolfie.* Alfred, we can register him. He's a Status Indian.

ALFRED: So?

RITA: He can be a member of the band. Maybe he is already.

ALFRED: Rita, his birth parents weren't from this band. We have no idea where—

RITA: We raised him here. He's the adopted grandson of a man who was a great friend to their people. Do you see? Our Wolf. They have to let *him* live here. This solves everything. My god! I'm such a mother to him I don't even see him as Indian anymore. But he is, Alfred. And he so desperately *wants* to be. And all the effort and sacrifices we've made raising him, the . . . the *hardships* . . . it's all going to pay off now, it's all going to come to something after all!

RITA sees WOLFIE in his hiding spot. Their eyes meet. He is heartbroken. He starts backing away.

          Oh! Wolfie! My son, my child. I could just squeeze him to death. Don't we just love him, Alfred? And Asta, you've been so good to him. Such a loving auntie. Come on, come on, you two. Let's go share this good news with him.

WOLFIE runs off.

          (sing-song) Wol-fie!

RITA starts inside and trips on something. ALFRED and ASTA catch her.

ALFRED: Sit down, Rita. You need to sit down.

RITA: Lemme go, we have to celebrate.

ASTA: I'll get you some water.

RITA: There's wine left. And get the maccers
               started. Freddie and I are going out.

*ASTA goes inside the kitchen for the water. Once seated,
RITA starts crying. Joy, sorrow, we don't know. ALFRED
tends to her.*

*Inside, ASTA notices blood on the wall where WOLFIE was
hiding. She sees blood drops nearby on the floor, lead-
ing off.*

ASTA: Wolfie, you're tracking blood every-
               where. Wolf!

ASTA goes off in search of WOLFIE.

               (offstage) Wolfie? *(and farther off)* Wolfie!

She returns and heads to the garden.

               He's not here. He's not in the cabin.

ALFRED: He's probably in the driveway or
               something.

ASTA: No.

ALFRED: Go around front again. I'll double around
               back.

*ASTA goes back through the kitchen and exits. ALFRED exits
the garden. We watch RITA sitting in the garden, listening
to their calls.*

               (offstage) Wolf! Where are you? Stop play-
               ing games!

ASTA: *(offstage)* Wol-fie? Come out come out wherever you are! Wolfie!

They converge again in the garden.

ALFRED: He knows he's not supposed to wander off.

ASTA: The longhouse? Janice invited him down.

ALFRED: That must be it. *(to RITA)* You all right, Rita? Asta and I'll go look for him.

ASTA: No, you stay with her, Freddie. I'll run down and find him. Don't worry. He can't be far.

ALFRED: You're right. Thanks, Asta.

ASTA runs off.

               She's right. He'll be down there. He was asking about it on our walk this morning. He's really taken an interest.

But RITA is still distraught.

               He's fine, Rita. He's not going to climb up into the mountains. He wouldn't get ten feet without breaking an ankle. Get a hold of yourself.

RITA: I can't. I won't.

ALFRED: What do you mean you won't.

RITA: This is my home. This is part of me.

ALFRED: Rita. We can work something out. It's not like that woman came by with an eviction notice. Like you said, she came to us for help. That means she sees us as neighbours, as part of the community. She doesn't see us as . . . encroachers or squatters to be got rid of. You see?

RITA: Hold me, Alfred. Just hold me.

ALFRED puts his arm around RITA.

What have I done?

ALFRED: Hey. You got into it with her a little but we can apologize for that. We can make it up to her.

The sound of a car approaching. Horn beeping urgently.

That must be her ride.

RITA: What have I done, Alfred? What have I done?

Voices off. Frantic shouts and cries.

ALFRED: What was that? Was that Asta?

RITA: Oh my god. Oh my god. Alfred . . .

ALFRED: ASTA! WOLFIE! *(to RITA)* Wait here.

He starts off. RITA clutches at him.

RITA: Stay with me. Please . . .

ALFRED: Rita. Let me go.

RITA: *No . . . No . . . No . . .*

ALFRED: Rita . . .

ASTA enters, breathless.

ASTA: He took off! Freddie! We have to go after him!

ALFRED: Took off where?

ASTA: Up the creek bed. The natives saw him. He ran in front of their truck and he took off.

ALFRED: Fuck—what is he thinking? That whole slope is a fucking debris field. Come on, Rita. We gotta get him before he hurts himself.

ALFRED and ASTA start off.

Rita! *(and as he exits)* Wolfie!

RITA: It's no use, Alfred. It's no use.

As the lights fade, WOLFIE enters like an apparition, disoriented, absolutely drenched to the skin as at the top of the show.

Black. Music.

ACT II

ain. Lost in themselves in separate areas of the
'A, BORGHEJM, ALFRED.

It was like a movie, they all say.

A mentally handicapped native youth . . .
Missing since Friday . . .

ALFRED remembers something, grieves over it.

BORGHEJM: There I am running toward the bridge,
hoofing it past all the cars stuck on
Dollarton, and in every car I see the glow
of the little screens, everybody watching
it all go down . . .

RITA: Search crews believe they have located . . .

ALFRED filled with anger and remorse.

Located but were unable to retrieve . . .
were unable to retrieve . . .

BORGHEJM: The fog of war they call it. The fog of war.
Means men with weapons in their hands
fucked things up. Means somebody got
killed who wasn't supposed to.

ALFRED cries out.

Oh, Jordan . . .

RITA: Wolfie . . .

BORGHEJM: In the fog of war, they can't see you for what you are—just a scared kid. All they see is your combat boots, your camo pants, your shirt that says, "Warrior Up!" All they see is your skin. All they see is the cardboard poster tube with your protest banner rolled up inside. To them it's a weapon, a pipe bomb.

RITA: Why, Wolf?

BORGHEJM: Why, Jordan? Why didn't you put it down, they say? Why didn't you put it down like they told you?

RITA: What did you think you were doing running off like that?

BORGHEJM: I know. *I know.* You're holding this thing, this banner, this thing you wanna say to them and show them. It's not a weapon but it's your defence, your ghost shirt, your whole reason for being on that bridge in the first place. How could you put it down? So you hold it out to them. See? *See?*

RITA: Was it about . . . being native? Trying to be like Grampa? Trying to be . . . what . . . ?

BORGHEJM: They'll never know who fired the tasers, how many. Why you holed up in the bus and screamed the things they say you did. They'll never know who fired the tear gas, and why you ran like an animal. They'll never know if you fell or jumped or were pushed over the edge. They'll never know cuz they conjure up the fog of war to hide those truths.

RITA: How, Wolfie? How did you wind up in the water where they say they found you? Did you fall in? Were you swept out? Did you . . . ? Was it really you they saw?

BORGHEJM: I see you falling, Jordan, falling forever now like the First Man of our people. Great Spirit told him to dive from a cliff into the waters of Indian Arm. From the bottom of the water he brought forth two handfuls of clay and made an island. In its place the next day, he saw a beautiful maiden walking the earth.

Lights out on RITA and BORGHEJM. The rain stops. ASTA enters and sees ALFRED.

ASTA: Freddie. I've been looking all over for you.

ALFRED shrugs as if to say: here I am.

You weren't here ten minutes ago.

ALFRED: . . .

ASTA: I wish you wouldn't wander around.

ALFRED: . . .

ASTA: Come back to the cabin, please? Rita needs you.

ALFRED: What does it matter? What does it matter now?

ASTA: She needs you. Freddie?

But ALFRED has gotten up and is staring at the trees all around.

67

ALFRED:	It's out here, Asta. Your father's trail. Not that I can find it. But Wolfie did. There's no other way he could've got up that far north. We never gave him credit for anything. *(pause)* It's karma.
ASTA:	What are you saying?
ALFRED:	We were on the verge of a new life. Wolfie, on the cusp of realizing his potential. Rita, for maybe the first time in her life, coming out from under her father's shadow. And me, ready to be a dad. And at the precise moment when we're poised as a family to make this great leap forward . . .
ASTA:	It's not karma.
ALFRED:	It's punishment. Cosmic retribution. We were never parents. Rita, incapable of real love because she's too needy herself. Me, with my selfish pursuit of literary . . . whatever, *art* . . . whatever you want to call it. And just days ago on the retreat I'd made a realization about the folly of it. The self-centred futility. And I rush back to my family, my son, to help him become all that he could be, and in that very instant . . .
ASTA:	You're being self-centred *now*. This happened to all of us. I'm grieving, too. We need to be together right now. You need to be with Rita.
ALFRED:	And do what? Watch her wallow in a drunken stupor?
ASTA:	She isn't drinking, it's all she can do to get out of bed. Can't you be generous

	with her, Freddie? Can't you be gener-ous with each other?
ALFRED:	We're not like you, Rita and me. When Wolfie first came into our lives you were what, nine, ten? So young. Yet you were like a mother to him at times. More than Rita ever was.
ASTA:	Rita is a wonderful mother. You said so yourself—
ALFRED:	She did a good job. Mothering. You're different, Asta. I look at you and I see nothing but genuine love and caring and goodness.
ASTA:	That's how we all need to be with each other. Now especially—
ALFRED:	Could you heal me, I wonder. If we were together, would I be healed by your good-ness? Or would I corrupt you?
ASTA:	You're a good man, Freddie. You just have to—
ALFRED:	You're beautiful.
ASTA:	Stop it.

She moves away from him.

	This isn't going to heal you.
ALFRED:	What.
ASTA:	Whatever it is you think you want from me.

ALFRED: You healed Wolfie. He came alive around you.

ASTA: Love healed Wolfie.

ALFRED: I need love.

ASTA: So does Rita. Go to her, please. Be with her. Talk to her. She lost Papa just a few months ago. She spent the whole summer worrying about losing the cabin. That alone was killing her. And now . . . She can't lose you, too, Freddie. Help her.

ALFRED: I can't.

ASTA: You have to try.

ALFRED: It's no use.

Silence. ALFRED *softly sings the refrain from "The Boxer" to himself.*

"Lie-la-lie . . . Lie-la-lie-lie-lie-la-lie . . . "

ASTA: *(taken aback)* Why are you singing that? Why was Wolfie singing that the other night?

ALFRED: *(speaks)* "All lies and jest. Still, a man hears what he wants to hear. And disregards the rest." It's a joke Wolf and I had. For when someone's not listening. To reason.

ASTA: Oh my god . . .

ALFRED: I don't mean you.

ASTA: I dreamt this. Three days ago. The morning I came up here.

ALFRED: This? Us here, right now?

ASTA: Yes.

ALFRED: The dream you said you forgot?

ASTA: I never forgot. *(pause)* We were in the waiting room at Sunny Hill, you and me, while Wolfie had his therapy. The nurse comes, we go in, and instead of the doctor's office we're here in this clearing. And instead of the doctor there's an elder, like a native elder, you know? And she says Wolfie's "the one." Wolfie starts freaking out, screaming, "She's lying! She's lying!" And then these other natives come in through the trees with a big scary knife and they hold him down and . . . they shave his head. And all over his head, tattooed into his scalp, there's like . . . a map, a chart, with stars and symbols and . . . and we're all just staring at this thing in awe and Wolfie's shaking, absolutely terrified, but then the elder gets a mirror and shows him, and this expression of pure joy comes over his face. And he says, "Okay. You found me." And then we all join hands in a circle around him and we start singing. *"Lie-la-lie . . ."*

ALFRED: My god.

ASTA: Why didn't I tell you guys? If only I'd told you . . .

ALFRED: What difference would it have made?

ASTA: It felt like a premonition. All that day I felt it. This dream, Jordan on the bridge, and then Wolfie and Janice. They were talking about Papa's trail and how he was going to find the Lost Island. If only I'd said something to him—like, hey, this isn't *Minecraft*, Wolf—or if only I'd told you, maybe we would've been more careful and Wolfie wouldn't have run off and—

ALFRED: Asta. You're not to blame. It was just a dream—

ASTA: Was it? Maybe we need to listen. Maybe there's something bigger than us that's trying to tell us something. And if we only listened. I try to be a good person, I try to live the right way, I just wish it meant more. I wish my actions were more than a fucking lifestyle choice.

ALFRED: No, no, no, you *are* good. You *do* listen. You live from the heart. You gave Wolfie love. The love he needed from his mother. Even this dream—don't you see—it came from your love. But Rita wasn't in it. You didn't want to tell it in front of her. Because *you know*. Subconsciously you know how she felt about him—

ASTA: Maybe she was the elder.

ALFRED: Oh sure. Like when she thought he was "indigo"? *That's* a fucking lifestyle choice. She bought every shred of horseshit about indigo children because that's the only way she could assuage her guilt over what she did to him. And muster any affection for him. He had to be gifted

	in some way. A member of some fucking New Age master race—
ASTA:	No! She was trying to understand him. Trying to figure out how to be a mother to him—
ALFRED:	You know how she feels. She saved him when he was a baby and she's regretted every—
ASTA:	STOP! LIE-LA-LIE!
ALFRED:	. . .
ASTA:	Who are you to judge, Freddie? Who are you to talk about my sister that way and take the memory of my nephew and shit all over it with your cynicism and cruelty?
ALFRED:	This is why I need you, Asta.
ASTA:	We all need each other. We need to take care of each other. Please. Let's go up together. You must be hungry. Freddie? Come on. I'll make you and Rita some lunch.
ALFRED:	Oh Jesus . . .

He is suddenly overcome.

	I forgot about him. Just now. I started thinking about what I wanted to eat and he completely left my mind. Fuck me! *Fuck me!*
ASTA:	Freddie . . . Hush . . . You're allowed—

ALFRED: I'm not! I'm not—don't you see? It's all I
            have that's good, that's not cynical and
            cruel. I can't forget. Not for an instant.

ASTA: You don't have to punish yourself like this.

ALFRED: Yes I do. I'm weak. My love is weak. All
            it takes is the thought of lunch—the
            normalcy of it!—and he's gone. Like he
            never existed.

ASTA: People need to rest from their grief.

ALFRED: What right do I have to rest? I'd rather
            drown in it. I'd rather drown!

He gets up abruptly, starts heading off.

ASTA: Where are you going? Freddie!

*She stops him. At her touch he immediately softens and
crumples into her. He falls to his knees. He buries his
face in her belly.*

ALFRED: There's nothing left for me.

RITA approaches the clearing.

ASTA: Shhh . . . You'll get through this. You still
            have Rita. Your work. You'll write again.
            I heard Wolfie say you're writing about
            Papa and the Lost Island. You'll do it one
            day, won't you? To honour their memory
            and do us all proud . . .

ALFRED: If only you'll help me. Give me strength.
            You're an angel, Asta. You're a comfort to
            me. A respite. You can heal me. You can
            save me.

ASTA: It's Rita you need.

ALFRED: I'll blame her. I'll say things I can't take
          back. Let me stay with you. Take me
          away somewhere. Another world, just
          the two of us. Somewhere I can start over
          and stand on my own two feet again . . .
          Nicaragua . . . Asta, take me away to
          Nicaragua—

ASTA: Freddie, shhh—

ASTA sees RITA.

          Come on. Get up.

ALFRED sees RITA, also. He picks himself up. Silence.

ALFRED: What are you doing here?

RITA: What am *I* doing?

ALFRED: Asta and I were talking.

RITA: So I see. I sent her to look for you. I
          don't know where you are. You sneak
          into the cabin in the middle of the night
          and you're gone again before the sun
          comes up.

ALFRED: . . .

RITA: I've been worried.

ALFRED: Worried. Is that what you were?

RITA: What else would I be?

ALFRED: Relieved—I was gone? Hopeful—I
          wouldn't return?

ASTA: For goddsakes. I'm going back to the cabin. I'm going to heat up some soup and I want the two of you back there in fifteen minutes.

ALFRED: Asta—

ASTA: Please. Work it out.

ASTA leaves. RITA and ALFRED stand in silence, some distance apart.

RITA: I can't get him out of my head. Can you?

ALFRED: I don't want to.

RITA: I mean the thought of them finding him like they did. Floating just below the surface. And then losing him again, as if something pulled him away, some current or . . . undertow. Like the water wouldn't give him up. I keep seeing his face, his eyes . . . Looking up at me. I see his lips move, he starts to say something, and then . . .

ALFRED: . . .

RITA: I don't know how you can bear to sit here with the Arm so close.

ALFRED: I want to be close.

RITA: But with those boats out there with their hooks and chains . . .

ALFRED: . . .

RITA: Freddie?

ALFRED: When you look into his eyes, Rita, is it recrimination that you see?

RITA: Don't. Please—

ALFRED: Is he accusing you? Is that what's haunting you?

RITA: What about you, Alfred? Why are you wandering the woods at every hour of the day and night?

ALFRED: My heart is broken.

RITA: Mine, too.

She wants to reach out to him, touch him, but he snorts derisively.

I come down here, I see you clutching at my baby sister, your face buried in her belly. And you can't so much as look at me. Am I so completely revolting to you?

ALFRED: You're as beautiful as the moment I first laid eyes on you. But your disappointments? Your resentment? The soul-crushing guilt you bear? Guilt masquerading as grief—

RITA: Masquerading?

ALFRED: Yes.

RITA: That's what you think of our lives together? Our family, our marriage? I devoted my life to you and Wolf. I loved—

ALFRED: You resented every living moment of his life. Even when he was a baby, even before the accident—

RITA: Don't you dare—

ALFRED: All you wanted was to live up to some ideal of your father's, be some glorious saviour to a poor native child, but you couldn't even bare to hold him—

RITA: Don't you fucking—

ALFRED: The minute we got him you wanted him gone. You said as much, you wished he was gone—

RITA: No! I never . . . I only wished . . . Alfred . . . Why couldn't we love him together? Why did loving him mean you had to pull away from me? I only ever wished he didn't come between us.

ALFRED: Well you got your wish, didn't you?

RITA: How can you . . . I wanted us to be a family—

ALFRED: A family? A family is bonded by love. We are supposed to love our child together, as parents, as mother and father—

RITA: Don't talk to me about love. I raised him. I saved his life and nurtured him back to health. I gave him the love and attention he needed. You spent most of Wolfie's life cloistered in your den, pecking away at your magnum opus. Sure you'd come out now and then, ten minutes here, ten minutes there, shower him

INDIAN ARM

with fun and affection, but we know who your real baby was. Only now that you've failed, failed as a writer, now you want to pretend—

ALFRED: You trying to hurt me, Rita? Everything I write gets published. *Everything.*

RITA: Oh, sure. Magazine articles. Op-eds. Reviews of other people's books. Where's your book, Alfred, your baby? I mean, you win the GG, then your second novel's a complete fucking mess, but, hey, sophomore jinx, right? So where's your comeback? When do you live up to your "early promise"? Is it the book you're writing now? The one you went on the retreat to work on? Oh, wait, you didn't write a word while you were away. Not a single word. Why is that?

ALFRED: If you don't get it, I can't explain it to you.

RITA: Oh I get it, Alfred. It's huge, right? A cathedral? Your Sistine Chapel? Let me guess—is it about my dad and the Lost Island? Yeah, I heard Asta talking about that. What a laugh. You with your MacBook and your energy drinks trying to write about blood and dirt and the whole fucking universe. My father had more passion, more pure animal force in the callouses of one hand than you will ever have in the entirety of your life and being.

ALFRED: Are you finished?

RITA: *You're* finished. That's the realization you made. Finished as a writer. So you come back and decide you'll try your hand at being a daddy and turn Wolfie into your next project. Your masterpiece. But not out of love, Alfred. No. As a reflection of you. That's all Wolfie was, that's all I ever was. We're just things you acquired to conform to some image of yourself. The artist, the good liberal, with the adopted native child and the beautiful wife, "we, who had the gold and the green forests." You look inside and tell me it isn't true.

Silence. ALFRED *is so enraged he could strike* RITA *or go off on a tirade of his own. He closes in on her ominously.* RITA *stands her ground and braces for the onslaught.*

ALFRED: Look at what you've become, Rita. You're ugly. Ugly and evil. Your soul is as barren as your womb—

RITA: You despicable . . . *You're* barren, a desert! You're a human wasteland—

ALFRED: Oh, yeah, keep going, keep going! Beautiful Rita. Beautiful, fuckable Rita! Look what misery and remorse have done to you!

RITA: At least I feel remorse. When you were the one who—

ALFRED: *I*? *I*—

RITA: You were the one who left him—

ALFRED: Because you—

RITA: You left the baby—

ALFRED: You pulled me into the bedroom, onto the bed—

RITA: You left the baby in the car!

ALFRED: Because you needed to fuck.

RITA: So did you.

ALFRED: "I need you, I need you," that's what you said, over and over.

RITA: And you said, "yes," and you said, "yes," and you lost yourself—

ALFRED: Because of you.

RITA: You abandoned yourself—

ALFRED: Because of you.

RITA: In love.

ALFRED: In fucking.

RITA: Because I needed you, for one moment in the day, to be out of your head, to not be a million miles away fretting over your precious words—

ALFRED: You see—it was your fault! Your fault—

RITA: You're horrid! You're the one who's horrid and ugly and evil!

ALFRED: You made me forget.

RITA: You left him in the car. In the sun. To burn and swelter.

ALFRED: You made me forget.

RITA: I saved him. I wrapped him in wet towels.
                     I breathed life into his little body . . .

ALFRED: Oh god . . . Wolfie . . . Poor Wolfie . . .

They grieve. Together, apart.

                     This is our karma, Rita. We went through
                     the motions of loving a child. Why? For
                     the experience? Your father's approval?
                     And afterward . . . Did we ever really love
                     him or was it just remorse?

RITA: I loved him. I loved you. I am a loving
                     person. You will never pervert that. You
                     will never take that away from me.

ALFRED: Is that what you think I've done?
                     Perverted your love?

RITA: I tried so hard to love you. I worried over
                     it and picked at it like a bloody sore.

ALFRED: . . .

RITA: What happened to us?

ALFRED: . . .

RITA: Don't you have anything to say?

ALFRED: I should follow Wolfie down. Make my
                     peace with him. If I knew I could find
                     him, I would do it. I would fling myself
                     over the edge like that boy on the bridge.

RITA: You're not at all like that boy. You just
                     want to escape.

ALFRED: Don't you?

RITA: That's not our karma, is it?

ALFRED: You think you can heal from this? Do
            your penance? Redeem yourself?

RITA: Stop. Please.

ALFRED: What.

RITA: Stop attacking me.

ALFRED: I'm attacking you? You should never have
            come down here. You should just let me
            go. You're better off without me.

RITA: Alfred. Why can't we help each other? Be
            loving to one another and heal ourselves.

ALFRED: Look at us, Rita. There's no redemption
            for us. We're poison together. Maybe we
            always were.

RITA: We were beautiful once. Alive. Full of hope
            and promise. The whole world before us.

ALFRED: I don't remember anymore.

RITA: Your "Jesus Year." That's what you
            called it. You were the son of God, the
            next CanLit star. I was a flower child, a
            rainbow warrior with a hatful of David
            Suzuki, and you made me your queen.
            You worshipped me with your words and
            your eyes and your body and I revelled
            in it. At summer's end we took Papa's old
            two-stroke and snuck onto the grounds
            of the Wigwam Inn. We lay on a blan-
            ket under the stars and you fingered

and sucked and rocked me until I came and came. It was endless, *endless*, I disappeared, I merged with the night, the pull of the earth, the tides, the weight of the air all around. And in the darkness, from the distance of starlight, I heard your voice. "All I need is you, Rita. You here with your forests and waters and sky. There's history here for a thousand and one nights. Just let me fuck you five times a day and I'll write a novel a year for the rest of my life." "God, yes," I said. "Forever. Take me forever."

ALFRED: Lovely Rita. Lovely ineffable Rita . . . *(starts laughing)* Or should I say *eff*-able. *Eff*-able Rita! Of course! The things you can do with language, eh! I mean, *ineffable*, sacred beyond words, and *eff*-able—

He can't speak for laughing.

And that's you in a word, isn't it, Rita? That's all you ever wanted or aspired to be—

RITA: Stop.

ALFRED: A good hot fuck! A totally *eff*-able, *(spells)* F-A-B-L-E, fable queen!

RITA: No. You're wrong, you're—

ALFRED: Why don't we try doing it in the road again? In the car so you can imagine it's him with the blue tape? Or better yet, right here. Just like old times.

He grabs her, starts groping her obscenely.

You condemned us, Rita—me, Wolfie, yourself—you condemned us with your adolescent hunger for—what?—for your pussy to get wet, your mind to get blown and your heart to go pitter-pat—

She lashes out at him. They struggle.

RITA: Do it then! Destroy me—that's what you want! Beat me bloody, Alfred! Kill me! Kill me! Do it! Be a man and get it over with!

She starts to crumble. ALFRED lets her go. She falls to the ground, sobbing. He looks at her for a beat then turns away, as broken as she is. BORGHEJM and ASTA now appear at the edge of the clearing.

ASTA: Rita . . . ? Freddie . . . ?

ALFRED: . . .

RITA tries to gather herself together.

ASTA: Rita, are you all right?

RITA: Yeah. Fine.

Her eyes meet BORGHEJM's. Neither gives an inch.

ASTA: I ran into her on the way to the cabin.

BORGHEJM: My condolences.

RITA: Likewise. We're sorry for your loss.

An uncomfortable silence. It is as if RITA expects BORGHEJM to leave.

ASTA: Janice . . . can you tell us what's happening with the investigation? Have they been able to find Jordan?

BORGHEJM: They found the banner he was going to hang. The police have it.

ASTA: Do you know what it was?

BORGHEJM: He took two street banners—you know the ones from the main res—our tribal banner with the wolf. He took two of those and put strips of cloth going across between them. And on the strips he painted the words respect, redemption, and reconciliation.

ASTA: I'm so sorry.

BORGHEJM nods her thanks to ASTA, then turns to RITA.

BORGHEJM: We're all grieving. And I come up here cuz this land means something to me, my family, my people. But you're looking at me like I'm trespassing.

RITA: My father—

BORGHEJM: I knew him better than you did.

RITA: Then you know this was his home as much as it is yours.

BORGHEJM: Yeah, but he understood something you don't. "Nothing belongs to you of what there is. Of what you take you must share." Chief Dan George said that right up there by the cabin the day my brother leased his allotment to your dad. And Erik understood. But you? You're the spoilt brat at the party who licks all the brownies. *You're* the one trespassing. *(to* ALFRED*)* You explained that to her, right? What those papers mean?

ALFRED *nods.*

Well, like I said, we're all grieving now. We'll deal with this in the fall.

BORGHEJM *starts off. As she is about to disappear into the woods:*

RITA: Wait. I want you to know something about me. Will you listen? Please?

BORGHEJM *waits.*

RITA: This isn't me. Who you think I am. Who I've become. I was my father's daughter oncc. The woman that you see now—I don't even recognize her. I'm so ashamed. And I feel so unworthy . . . of this land . . . my Papa's cabin . . . and Wolfie . . . Poor Wolfie . . .

ASTA *moves to comfort* RITA.

ASTA: Rita . . .

RITA: Take it. Take it away from me. I want to be free now. I want to be free of it. Just take it away! Tear it down! Tear it all down!

ASTA: Rita, please. Hush now—

RITA: Tear it down and put everything back the way it was.

BORGHEJM: The way it was?

RITA: The land. Everything. I've carried this burden, the guilt of living here all my life. *(to ASTA)* So did Papa, Asta. That's why he spent half his life trying to disappear. I don't want that to happen to me. I'm leaving. I'm leaving right now—

ASTA: What are you talking about?

RITA: Yes.

ASTA: Freddie? What—

RITA: Freddie doesn't matter anymore.

ASTA: Rita. *(to BORGHEJM)* I'm sorry. I think we need to be alone right now.

RITA: No. *(to BORGHEJM)* You're right. I took something of yours that wasn't mine to take and it ruined me. It ruined everything. I'm sorry it's in shambles but I want to give it back to you. Will you accept? Take back what I can give you—

BORGHEJM: You're your father's daughter all right.

RITA: Yes. I am. Can you see that?

BORGHEJM: What I mean is, to say you want to undo the past, go back to some unsullied time . . . Erik said those same things to me a long time ago. Right here in these woods. Going on fifty years ago now . . .

ASTA: Fifty years ago? So he didn't want the lease? He wanted to give it back to you?

RITA: The sixties, Asta, the sixties happened. They leased Papa the land in 1959. And then Vietnam, the hippies. He brought drugs in here, who knows what. He felt he defiled this place. *(to BORGHEJM)* Isn't that right?

BORGHEJM: That was part of it.

RITA: This place is sacred to you. A healing place, a sanctuary.

BORGHEJM: Inlailawatash Reserve 2A. *2A*—like something they threw in as a bonus. But to us, yeah, it's the centre of something. Where our women and children came to hide in times of war. Where we came to heal in times of sickness.

RITA: And where you hid out when you were a girl. Hid from that school.

BORGHEJM: You're trespassing again.

RITA: Trespassing? *No.* This land belongs to you, but my father lived and died here. His story, his life, is a part of this place now. He was a friend to you, a brother. He helped your family and your community through a very dark time. He loaded up his truck with moms and dads and aunties and grandparents and drove them out to Keith Road to that school, drove them around and around the gates so they could call out "happy birthday" and sing to their children and bring news from home. And people spat at him. People treated him like he was committing some sort of abomination. But he kept on. And then? And then he saved

89

you. He literally marched through the gates, gathered you and your brothers and sisters—

BORGHEJM: STOP!

Silence.

This fairy tale you're telling—The Legend of Erik the Red and His Friendly Truck Loki—it's a whitewash. You're still trying to undo the past. You're taking my suffering, my family's suffering, and turning it into a pretty little myth like your dear old dad was Oskar fucking Schindler. Oh, he saved the poor native children and brought 'em back to the bush and they played in the sun and ate blackberries forevermore. The end.

RITA: It's not a pretty little myth. It's our family history. You have myths yourself which connect you to this land, myths about wolves and warriors and—

BORGHEJM: They connect us because they tell the whole truth. Yeah, we tell of a mother wolf finding a baby in the woods. Why was that baby left alone? Where were all the people? They were dead, that's what, wiped out by smallpox. You see? Our stories help us make sense of the world. But your so-called family history just tells about your dad's heroic victory over fucking St. Paul's Residential School. Sure I'm grateful he delivered us out from the evil of that place, but that's not the end of the story, is it? He couldn't deliver the evil of that place out from us. My brothers and sisters he "saved," they're all dead of booze and drugs and worse. And what about me? And what about him? What happened to us? Who's gonna tell that part of the story?

RITA: Tell me, then. Tell me the truth. Tell me about my father. Or would you prefer not to? What do you tell the kids up at that longhouse—that you were saved by wolves?

A standoff.

ASTA: Janice . . . I don't want to believe a lie. If you know the truth . . .

BORGHEJM and ASTA regard one another. But BORGHEJM looks away.

Won't you tell us?

BORGHEJM: Nothing more to tell. Like your sister said. Erik let a whole bunch of riff-raff come through here in the sixties. Hippies, draft dodgers, back-to-the-land types gettin' high, shittin' everywhere . . . rolling around naked like it was the Garden of Eden. Summer of Love . . .

ALFRED has been listening intently. He notices a shift in BORGHEJM's tone from reportage to personal memory.

ALFRED: Summer of Love, huh?

BORGHEJM: *(covering)* Until the hard drugs started coming in. Then Byron and the Chief come up here, Chief tells Erik a man has a responsibility to rise above the mud and the shit. And Erik . . . he was . . .

ashamed . . . ashamed to find himself grovelling in it . . . *(pause)* Anyways . . .

BORGHEJM heads off.

RITA: You were here for that Summer of Love.

BORGHEJM stops. Silence.

BORGHEJM: I used to paddle up here all the time.

ASTA: To see Papa . . . ?

BORGHEJM: I used to tell my mama I was gonna marry him when I grew up. When I was little, I was the sweetest singer anybody ever heard. "You sing so good, Janice," people would say to me. And the first time Erik ever heard me, the expression on his face made my heart swell up like a hot water bottle.

Then one day, I get put on the bus to that place. I never sang another note for the rest of my life without crying over everything I lost.

The last winter I got so sick. I was wasting away in the infirmary and the Mother Superior comes to me in the night and says, "You're gonna die here. I got an ugly little plot picked out for you by the corner of the fence."

I think I did die that night. I chased an eagle into the sky and away we went, past Grey Rocks and Hamber, the North Arm opening up like the gates to heaven. When I opened my eyes Erik was carrying me down the hallway, and my brothers and sisters were running out the doors to Loki, and I saw my mama sitting on the curb, crying so hard she couldn't stand.

We hid out here all through the spring until they tore the school down. Erik and Byron built up the cabin and all of us kids lived here for a while until Mama said it was time to live like humans again and brought us back to Dollarton. Byron went to the band and said, "I want to let Erik stay at Inlailawatash." They gave him the allotment, let him lease it out.

We'd come up to visit all the time, all us kids. And when I got a little older, got to be a pretty young thing, I'd paddle up here by myself. Just to see him . . .

She takes in the air, speaks to it.

You wanted so much to belong to this place, Erik, and I thought I could give that to you. Afterward when you were ashamed and repulsed and said we couldn't ever see each other again, I thought it was me you were ashamed of. Me you were repulsed by. We both had to run a long, long way, a long ways away from the world of people to get away from what we did. Been a long time getting back, eh?

She comes back to the others.

About the cabin . . . We don't want you to tear it down. We have the longhouse down the road now so . . . one idea is to turn your place into a healing centre for our youth. To honour your boy, and ours. So you know.

With a nod BORGHEJM *heads off.* ASTA *calls after her.*

ASTA: Janice? You sing good . . .

ASTA *looks to* RITA *and* ALFRED. *She exits, too, without a word.* ALFRED *and* RITA *regard one another.*

ALFRED: Goodbye, Rita.

RITA: Is it?

ALFRED: Yes.

RITA: What will you do with yourself?

ALFRED: I dunno. Endure? You?

RITA: I want to change.

ALFRED: That's good. Hold on to that.

RITA: I will. *I will.* I want to help people. If they turn the cabin into some sort of youth shelter or something, I'd love to be a part of that somehow. For Wolfie.

ALFRED: You?

RITA: I'd need time. Training.

ALFRED: You'd do that?

RITA: I want to.

ALFRED: Well. If this is more than a Sunday mood, you really have changed.

RITA: It's who I was. Before you. Before Wolfie. Before everything. I cared about the world. I believed in the world. I want to be that person again. Try at least.

ALFRED: You're not doing it to help anybody though. Just so we're clear.

RITA: Why am I doing it then?

ALFRED: Guilt again. Noblesse oblige.

RITA: Don't be that way, Alfred. You had ideals once. You believed in things—

ALFRED: Sandinista.

RITA: What?

ALFRED: I had a truck, like your dad. Beat up Chevy Blazer. I lent it to a photographer friend of mine one summer while I did a writing course back east. Was there about a month when I got this postcard. Spanish-looking buildings, palm trees. It said, "Hey, Fred, I came down to Nicaragua to shoot, left your truck on the street. Police took it. Sorry." Well. I'm thinking, awesome, the Sandinistas impounded my truck. And I'm picturing them driving around Managua in my Blazer, flags on the front, machine gun in the flatbed. Few weeks later, we meet up back in Vancouver and I'm like, "Oh, man, I can't believe you drove my Blazer all the way to Nicaragua!" And he goes, "Are you stupid? I left that piece of shit parked on Union Street and the cops towed it away." I spent that summer listening to the Clash and dreaming my truck was a Sandinista. And that's as close as I ever got to the revolution.

RITA: You'll write again, Alfred. And I'll be the first in line to buy your book.

ALFRED: Thank you.

RITA: If there's one thing we can take away from all this, it's that we can heal. We can forgive one another. Just think about the banner that boy made. Respect, redemption . . .

ALFRED: Reconciliation.

RITA: Reconciliation.

ALFRED: When will we start I wonder.

RITA: Tomorrow. Let's start tomorrow.

They let that sit for a beat.

ALFRED: I'm gonna grab a bite.

RITA: Yeah, yeah. I'll be there in a minute.

ALFRED exits. RITA gazes out into the distance.

"We, who had the gold and the green forests . . . "

RITA exits. We hear sparse music, a drum, a voice. WOLFIE now appears as at the beginning of the play: drenched, breathing heavily, missing his glasses. But as the scene progresses, he slowly transforms and becomes whole.

WOLFIE: Grampa? That you? Jordan? Hello? *(pause)* Is this it? Am I here? I found the trail.

I followed it. Picked it up at Thwaytes, climbed up Holmden Creek all the way to Elsay Lake. Cut through the bush to Coldwell, and then up, up, into the sky, over Silver Falls and Bishop's Peak. Past Spray of Pearls, I saw the shadow of an island out in the Arm and I followed the trail down.

He looks around.

So is this it? Am I here?

He listens to the music. He blinks and squints at something in the distance.

Wait . . . I see you . . . I see you! My elders, my people, all my relations . . . Hello! Let me join you!

He starts off but suddenly becomes self-conscious.

I'm sorry, I . . . When I was a baby . . . *(despairing)* How long I gotta be this way? You know. How long?

The music rises, triumphant. WOLFIE *takes stock of himself. Finding himself whole, his entire being swells with pride and exhilaration.*

Oh . . . I'm here! I'm here! I'm here!

Blackout.

THE END

Hiro Kanagawa is a Vancouver-based actor, playwright, screenwriter, and teacher. His distinctions include Jessie Richardson Theatre Awards for both acting and playwriting, an Asians on Film Award, and an MFA from Simon Fraser University. Among his numerous screen credits he is perhaps best known for his recurring roles and guest appearances on popular American television series such as *The X-Files*, *Smallville*, *iZombie*, and *The Man in the High Castle*. Behind the camera, he was story editor on the critically acclaimed Canadian series *Da Vinci's Inquest*, as well as *Da Vinci's City Hall*, *Intelligence*, and *Blackstone*. On stage, his previous plays include *Tiger of Malaya* (Factory Theatre, Toronto/National Arts Centre, Ottawa), and *The Patron Saint of Stanley Park* (Arts Club, Vancouver).

First edition: December 2016. Second printing: December 2017.
Printed and bound in Canada by Imprimerie Gauvin,
Gatineau

Cover art by Kristen Johnson, cover photo by Wendi Wirawan

**PLAYWRIGHTS
CANADA PRESS**
202-269 Richmond St. W.
Toronto, ON
M5V 1X1

416.703.0013
info@playwrightscanada.com
www.playwrightscanada.com

MIX
Paper from
responsible sources
FSC® C100212